TRADITIONAL CANDLE.

# Traditional Candlemaking

*Simple methods of manufacture*

DEBORAH MILLINGTON

INTERMEDIATE TECHNOLOGY PUBLICATIONS 1992

Published by Intermediate Technology Publications,
103–105 Southampton Row, London WC1B 4HH, UK.

© Intermediate Technology Publications 1992

ISBN 1 85339 124 7

Typeset by Inforum, Rowlands Castle, Hants
Printed by S.R.P. Exeter

# Contents

**Introduction**                                                    vii

1. **Materials**                                                      1
   The fuel                                                          1
   The wick                                                          6

2. **Melting the fuel**                                              11
   Heating equipment                                                11
   Methods of measuring and controlling temperature                 12

3. **Candlemaking techniques**                                      15
   Dipping                                                          25
   Pouring                                                          28
   Moulding (or casting)                                            30

4. **Producing decorative candles**                                 35
   Dyeing                                                           35
   Painting                                                         35
   Dried flowers and grasses                                        35
   Carving                                                          36

**Appendices**                                                      37
   I     Common problems                                            37
   II    Conversion factors                                         39
   III   Suppliers of raw materials and equipment                   39

# Acknowledgements

IT Publications and the author would particularly like to thank Mr David Constable of Candle Makers Supplies, 28 Blythe Road, London W14, for all his help and advice, and for permitting us to take photographs used in this book.

The author would also like to thank the following people and organizations for their assistance while preparing this book: Prices Patent Candle Company Ltd, Battersea, London; Ian Johnson (Technical Service Manager) Unichem Chemicals Ltd; Sandy Wareing and Workers at Botton Village, Danby, North Yorkshire and the Ironbridge Gorge Museum Trust, Ironbridge, Telford, Salop.

# Introduction

A candle is a solid cylinder of fat or wax enclosing a wick which can be burnt to give light. Candles have been made since the earliest times, and it is still possible to make them by well-established methods requiring only simple equipment, much of which can be made by rural artisans.

This book divides candlemaking into three main areas: the materials needed, the methods of melting the fuel, and the techniques for enclosing the wick in the fuel. These areas are not completely separate from one another — decisions taken in one have an effect on other areas. The book aims to cover a wide a range of possibilities in each of the three areas, recognizing that there are as many different situations as there are people making candles. For this reason, guidance is given on a range of options rather than specific instructions relating to a single situation. Experimentation is important – good candles can only be produced by trial and error!

Details of a number of companies which supply raw materials and/or equipment for use in candlemaking are given in Appendix III. It must be emphasized, however, that there are many more suppliers than can be mentioned here, and it is advisable to purchase goods from a local supplier if this is possible.

## Why make candles?

Candles have been used in many parts of the world to provide the main source of light, to provide additional lighting which is softer than electric light, in religious ceremonies and for timekeeping. Despite the invention of the electric light bulb, candles are still in demand.

As a source of light, candles have a number of advantages in that they are relatively cheap, self-contained and portable and can thus be used when or where other kinds of lighting are unavailable. In addition to utilitarian candles, decorative candles can be produced in an endless variety of sizes, shapes and colours.

In terms of manufacture, candles are produced on every scale, from individually in the home to mass production in large, automated factories. For the small-scale producer, candles can be produced relatively easily using simple equipment which can be made by local tradespeople. The costs of setting up a small-scale candlemaking venture need not be high. In addition, if local suppliers of raw materials suitable for candlemaking are sought out, raw material costs can be minimized and the local economy benefits.

The candles produced can be as simple or ornate as required — depending on their end-use. The technique may be as straightforward or complicated as necessary to produce the desired effect. Using the techniques outlined in this book, good quality utilitarian and decorative candles can be produced relatively easily. Once these techniques have been mastered, the scope for experimenting with new materials, processes and equipment is enormous.

# 1. Materials

## The fuel

It is important to select a fuel which is both appropriate for a particular situation and which produces a good candle (that is one which burns steadily, lasts for a long time, produces very little smoke and gives a good quality light). The wax should also be able to support the wick in a vertical position (which may prove to be a problem in hotter climates), be suitable for processing by one of the various candle making techniques, and look attractive.

Many modern candles are made from a mixture of paraffin wax and stearine, often with small quantities of other waxes added for the sake of appearance. Although this may be suitable in many situations, there are many other substances which can also be used as fuel for candlemaking, some of which are mentioned below.

### Paraffin wax

Paraffin wax is the most important raw material used in candlemaking. It is a by-product of the petroleum industry, being separated out from crude oil during distillation, and is usually supplied by petrol refining companies.

Fully refined paraffin waxes, which are ideal for candlemaking, are translucent to opaque in appearance, colourless, odourless, tasteless and hard or firm in consistency at room temperature. They have a melting-point range of 46° to 68°C. Those waxes which melt at around 58°C are ideal for candlemaking in temperate climates, although wax with a higher melting point is required for use in hotter climates. It is also possible to make candles using semi-refined paraffin waxes although this diminishes the quality of the end product.

Paraffin wax may be used to make candles by any of the techniques described in Chapter 3. However, in certain cases it may prove necessary to add other materials to the paraffin wax to make up the final candle composition. This is especially true in hotter climates, where paraffin wax candles have a tendency to bend, because they are unable to support their own weight. This problem can be avoided by the addition of stearine, the proportion required being dependent on the circumstances (see below). Small quantities of high-melting-point waxes may also be added to harden the paraffin wax.

1

## Stearine

Stearine is a component of many animal and vegetable fats and has become an important material in candlemaking. It is, in fact, a mixture of palmitic and stearic acids, together with a small amount of unsaturated acid. The ratio of the acids present is dependent both on the raw material from which the stearine is produced and on the processing technique employed. Much of the stearine produced in Europe is made from animal fat (tallow), while that produced in south-east Asia is made from vegetable oil. Stearine is usually supplied by oil and chemical companies.

Stearine is important as a hardening agent for paraffin wax owing to its good temperature stability. It helps to overcome the problem of 'bending' which is sometimes experienced with paraffin wax candles in hotter climates, and also helps in the release of candles from moulds.

The amount of stearine to be used varies, depending on the quality of candle required. Although the average amount is about 10 per cent, up to 50 per cent may be required for candles in warmer climates. There are several other factors which need to be considered when deciding on the amount of stearine to be used:

○ stearine is an expensive material;
○ pure stearine candles can only be made by moulding;
○ when the proportion of stearine used is greater than about 40 per cent, much of the 'plastic' property of the wax blend is lost;
○ when the amount of stearine in a paraffin wax/stearine candle is between about 40 per cent and 60 per cent, the temperature stability of the candle may be affected. Without the addition of a very small quantity of high melting-point wax, it is possible that the melting-point of the paraffin/stearine blend will fall below 50°C;
○ given paraffin wax and stearine candles of comparable weight, paraffin wax candles give considerably more light than stearine candles (almost one-and-a-half times as much). This is due to the greater proportion of carbon in paraffin wax compared with stearine (which contains oxygen). The amount of light given out by a candle is dependent on the proportion of carbon present.

## Microcrystalline waxes

Microcrystalline waxes are, like paraffin waxes, by-products of the petroleum industry. They are obtained either from the distillation process itself or from crude oil tank bottoms and have a melting-point range of 60–93°C. Microcrystalline waxes can be split into two types, namely 'soft' or 'plastic' waxes which are ductile, pliable and slightly sticky, and 'hard' waxes which are quite brittle. The hard waxes in particular are used in very small quantities (up to one per cent) to improve the finished appearance of the candle. This is achieved by depositing a hard skin on the surface of the candle, making it shiny and resistant to minor damage. However, these waxes are very expensive and are not usually required in very simple methods of candlemaking.

## Beeswax

Beeswax, a relatively soft and sticky substance with a melting point of about 64°C, is obtained by melting the honeycomb of the bee in hot water, straining it and allowing it to cool. At this stage it is a brownish-yellow colour and is usually bleached before being used in candlemaking. Information on making and using a solar wax melter to melt the beeswax and separate it from impurities may be obtained from the University of California (address given in Appendix III).

Beeswax has been used in the manufacture of candles since the earliest times, and is an excellent material with which to make dipped and poured candles. However, it is unsuitable for use in the manufacture of moulded candles, since it undergoes considerable contraction on cooling and has a tendency to stick to the mould. Iron equipment should not be used in the processing of beeswax, as it results in contamination of the wax.

Beeswax is also a very expensive commodity, and candles made from it are considered a luxury. However, when added to paraffin wax in quantities of about 5 per cent it improves both the burning time and appearance of the candles.

## Tallow

Tallow is made from melted animal fat. It is rarely used in present-day candlemaking as it is greasy to the touch, creates an unpleasant odour when burning and does not provide as good a source of light as wax-based candles. Tallow can be used to make both dipped and moulded candles.

## Vegetable waxes

Many plants, shrubs and trees yield waxes which can be extracted, purified as necessary and used in the manufacture of candles. In some cases, it may be possible to use these waxes as the main source of fuel for the candle, in others it may only be possible to use them in small quantities to improve the qualities of another wax.

Table 1 lists a number of vegetable waxes which may be suitable for use in candlemaking, and their geographical locations. There

## Table 1.   Vegetable waxes and vegetable tallows

| Name of wax | Melting point °C | Country/region of origin | Comments |
|---|---|---|---|
| Candelilla | 60–73 | Mexico, USA | Colour of beeswax when warmed, burns with a bright flame. Increases hardness of candle when blended with paraffin wax without any great increase in melting point |
| Capeberry | 41–45 | South Africa | |
| Caranday | 80–85 | Brazil, Paraguay | Wax not exploited commercially |
| Carnauba | 83–86 | N E Brazil S Brazil N Argentina N Paraguay | Best quality wax is obtained from young leaves gathered 3 times between September and March. Used as a melting-point booster for paraffin waxes |
| Cauassu | 81–86 | Amazon Basin | Hardness comparable with carnauba wax |
| Cochin-China | 40 | Far East, Kampuchea, (similar trees found in Nigeria, West Africa) | Used for moulded candles |
| Colombian Palm | 93 | New Grenada, Colombia, Ecuador | Crude wax burns with clear, bright flame. Refined wax used as a replacement for carnauba |
| Gondang (Godang, Kondang, Getah, Java) | 60 (approx) | Warm and tropical regions eg. Java, Sumatra, Sri Lanka | Wax obtained from the oil liquid which separates on warming the sap |
| Japan | 45–53 | Japan, China, Indo-China, India | Rancid colour like animal tallow, Mixed with a considerable amount of paraffin wax to make candles |
| Myrtle | 45 | Central and South America | Used to make high grade candles and tapers |
| Ouricury | 82–83 | Honduras, along Amazon River, N Brazil, E Brazil | Dense, hard, brittle, yellow wax. Melting-point booster for paraffin waxes |
| Ucuhuba | 41–44 | Brazil, Panama, Guatemala, Venezuela | |

4

are, of course, many more in existence than can be mentioned here and it may be necessary to experiment with different waxes to see which ones are suitable for candlemaking.

## Other additives

### Dyes and pigments

It is more difficult to produce coloured candles than to produce ordinary white ones because of the problems outlined. The colouring materials fall into two basic categories, oil-soluble dyes and pigments.

Certain problems are associated with the use of oil-soluble dyes, namely: fading, colour migration into the packaging material and oxidation (in which a gradual colour change from standard takes place). A satisfactory appearance is more easily obtained using dark colours, and the dyes have no adverse effect on the burning properties of the candle.

Pigment colours are very bright and neither bleed nor fade on exposure to sunlight. However, as they do not dissolve to form a solution but remain suspended in the wax mixture as small particles, they tend to fall to the bottom of the container unless the mixture is stirred regularly. In addition, the particles may clog the wick, and so prevent the candle from burning properly.

Dyes and pigments for use in candlemaking may be bought either in powder or disc form from various suppliers.

It is, of course, possible to purchase only the primary colours (red, yellow and blue), and use these to prepare other colours as required. Although this practice can produce shades which may not be readily available from suppliers, accurate measuring equipment will be required in order to reproduce a colour consistently.

### Perfumes

The use of perfume in the manufacture of candles results in a pleasant odour while burning which may also prove useful, for example, as an insect repellent. Perfumed candles, however, are difficult to make, and usually do not burn well. In addition, all perfumes contain residues that do not burn completely and which slowly choke the wick, the proportion of residue being dependent on the particular perfume used.

Perfume oils may be bought from suppliers in various countries. However, there are also a large number of perfumes made from natural sources, some of which may be of use in candlemaking. It is a question of discovering which locally available perfume oils are suitable for use with candles.

5

## The wick

The type of wick originally used in candlemaking was made of bleached twisted cotton yarn (Figure 1). On burning, it stood upright in the centre of the flame (which is cool) and was therefore unable to burn away cleanly. The result was a very smoky flame, providing only dim light and requiring frequent snuffing. The wick used in modern candles is made of plaited or braided cotton (Figure 2), resulting in a uniform wick which curls as it burns. The curling

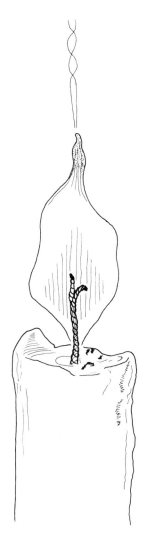

**Figure 1.** *Candle with twisted cotton wick*

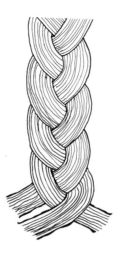

**Figure 2.** *Plaited cotton wick*

brings the end of the wick into the hottest part of the flame where it is able to burn away cleanly and thus provides a bright flame, with no need for snuffing (Figure 3).

When the wick is lit, the flame should radiate sufficient heat to melt a small pool of wax at the top of the candle. The liquid wax is then drawn up the wick by capillary action into the flame where it is vaporized and burnt. The size of the wick is important and should be related to the diameter of the candle and to the mixture of waxes used as fuel.

If the wick used is too thick, it causes a large flame to form, which generates so much heat that it prevents the formation of the pool of molten fuel by melting the outer edge of the candle and allowing the wax to run down the sides. On the other hand, if the wick used is too thin, the flame is unable to generate enough heat to form a proper reservoir of molten fuel. The result is that the flame burns a hole down the centre of the candle until it is extinguished through lack of oxygen. As a general rule, candles with large diameters require thicker wicks than those with small diameters.

Substances such as beeswax which are viscous when liquid require a thicker wick than substances with a lower viscosity. In general, the more viscous the liquid fuel, the thicker the wick required. In countries with established candlemaking industries, wicks may be obtained directly from manufacturers, or, in smaller quantities, from craft suppliers. It is also possible to make wicks by hand, using simple equipment.

7

**Figure 3.** *Candle with plaited cotton wick*

Many of the wicks which are made for use in large-scale industrial candle manufacture are three-strand plaits.[1] This is because, if high quality cotton is used in wick manufacture and the finished candle is to be made from high quality wax, a satisfactory wick may be obtained by plaiting with three strands. However, if high quality cotton is not available and/or the candle cannot be made from the finest quality wax, it may be necessary to use a braided wick for the larger diameter candles in particular. It is important to bear this in mind when either buying or making candle wicks.

---

[1] The terms 'plait' and 'braid' are commonly used interchangeably. To avoid confusion, wicks made from three strands will be referred to here as 'three-stranded plaits' (where a strand refers to the collection of ends of cotton which is used as a single unit during the plaiting process) while wicks made from four or more strands will be referred to as 'braids'.

After braiding (or plaiting) the wick is treated chemically. It is first bleached, then dampened out and soaked in a mordant solution (such as the one given below) for fifteen minutes. It is then dried in an open state (not wound or reeled).

*Mordant solution (100%)*

1.9%     Ammonium Phosphate
21.3%    Ammonium Sulphate
5.5%     Ammonium Chloride
0.35%    Potassium Chloride
70.95%   Water

As there are other factors which help to determine the size of wick required (including the composition of the wax mixture used and the effect of perfumes and colouring materials), it is only possible to give a rough guide to wick size in relation to the diameter of the candle (see Table 2). Each time candles of a new size or shape are to be produced, it is important to make a small number first to ensure that the correct wick size has been chosen.

The various suppliers specify their wicks in different ways; for example by the number of strands and numbers of ends in each strand (so that a 3 × 5 wick would be plaited from three strands, each of which contains five ends of cotton) or simply by the diameter of the candle for which it is intended.

### Table 2. Wick sizes

| Candle diameter in mm (inches) | Number of strands | Number of ends per strand | Number of plaits per cm. |
|---|---|---|---|
| 13/(0.5) | 3 | 5 | 6 |
| 25/(1) | 3 | 10 | 4.5 |
| 38/(1.5) | 3 | 15 | 4 |
| 51/(2) | 3 | 20 | 3.5 |
| 64/(2.5) | 3 | 25 | 3 |
| 76/(3) | 3 | 30 | 2.5 |
| 102/(4) | 3 | 35 | 2.5 |

# 2. Melting the fuel

In the manufacture of candles it is essential that the fuel being used is heated to the temperature required (which is dependent both on the fuel itself and on the process to be followed) and maintained at that temperature for the duration of manufacture. The equipment used for heating will depend on the source of heat available.

The most important aspect to be considered in the design and use of equipment is safety. It is important that the wax is not over-heated; heating above 150°C can result in unpleasant and dangerous fumes being given off. It is also very important to prevent wax from being spilt on to a naked flame as this would present a very serious fire hazard. These situations can be avoided, for example, by the use of a water jacket (Figure 4) in which the fuel is not heated directly but absorbs heat from the water surrounding it. This in itself may become a safety hazard if the water is allowed to boil away, so precautions must be taken to prevent this from happening.

## Heating equipment

### Electricity

Electricity is ideal as a source of heat if it is available, as it is easily controlled. Heating elements may be bolted to the bottom of a tank, or electrically-heated water jackets may be used.

### Gas

Tanks or pots may be placed on gas heaters provided that the bottom is thick enough to prevent the wax from burning. However, the use of a gas-heated water jacket may well be preferable to avoid the danger of spilling wax onto a naked flame.

### Solid fuel

Solid fuel should only be used where no other source of fuel is available. **Great care must be taken to prevent wax from being spilt onto naked flames.** Again, the best solution may well be that of a water jacket, this time heated by solid fuel. It may also be possible to use either a specially-constructed or a standard type of oven.

In all cases, containers to be used for melting the wax should be leakproof and made from steel, aluminium or iron (except in the case of beeswax, where iron equipment is not suitable). Copper and brass should be avoided as they cause oxidation.

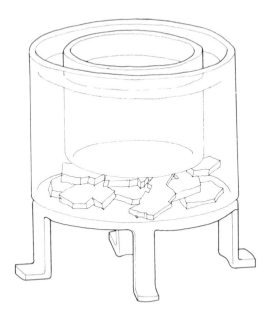

**Figure 4.**  *Use of a water jacket in heating the wax*

## Methods of measuring and controlling temperature

Although it is possible to make candles without any means of determining the temperature of the fuel, it is not advisable to do so as the likely result is the production of a high percentage of poor quality candles.

If it is available, a thermostat is a very good way of controlling the temperature of the wax, provided that it has been accurately calibrated. The use of a thermostat in conjunction with some form of electrical heating equipment allows the wax to be heated to a specified temperature and maintained at that temperature without the need for frequent manual checking and adjustment.

A thermometer is also a good way of measuring temperature although, in general, monitoring and adjustment have to be carried out manually. It is therefore important that, when using this method, the temperature of the wax mixture is checked frequently and adjusted as necessary. One of the advantages of thermometers is that they are relatively cheap and there are several types which may be used.

12

Thermometers for use in candlemaking should have a range of 0°C to 100°C. It is possible to use an ordinary mercury-in-glass thermometer, which is relatively cheap (and sufficiently accurate if it conforms to BS 1704:1985) or a sugar thermometer (used for bottling, jam-making etc.) It is also possible to purchase electrical contact thermometers which heat the wax until it reaches a specified temperature, and only start heating again when the temperature of the wax mixture has fallen. However, these thermometers are relatively expensive.

It is important that a thermometer is not heated beyond its upper limit as this is likely to make it very inaccurate in future.

# 3. Candlemaking techniques

There are three methods of candlemaking which are particularly suitable for small-scale manufacture, namely dipping, pouring and moulding (casting). The general principle and main area of use of each technique is outlined in brief here and examples of specific implementations of the techniques are given in greater detail later. Although other methods (such as compression and extrusion) exist, they tend to be used mainly by those candlemakers who wish to produce on a large-scale basis.

The methods described below allow candles of many different shapes and sizes to be produced, so that it is possible to make both utilitarian and decorative candles. The selection of a particular process will be dependent on the equipment and space available, and on the size, shape and quantity of candles to be produced, as well as the raw materials to be used.

**Dipping** is the simplest method of making candles. It consists of immersing the wick in molten wax and withdrawing it, so that it picks up wax as it emerges. The wax is allowed to cool and the process is repeated until the required candle thickness has been built up. The method enables several hundred candles to be produced in a day using relatively simple equipment. The length and diameter of candles produced by this method is limited only by the dimensions of the dipping can.

The **pouring** technique consists of suspending a wick over a container of molten wax and pouring the hot wax from a ladle so that it runs down the wick, cooling as it goes. Any surplus drips back into the main container and can be used again. This method uses the simplest equipment, but a fair degree of skill is required to produce good quality candles. The technique is used in particular for very long candles, where it would be very difficult to find a vessel deep enough for dipping.

The **moulding** (or casting) technique involves filling a mould (in which a wick has been positioned) with molten wax, allowing the wax to cool and then removing the completed candle from the mould. Unless this method is being used to produce a very small number of candles per day, a certain degree of sophistication in mould design and fairly large numbers of moulds are needed. Moulds may be rigid or flexible, but can be made only from certain materials. This technique enables candles of different shapes and sizes to be produced.

The following descriptions are examples of how these ideas can be translated into practice in terms of equipment and methods. It is

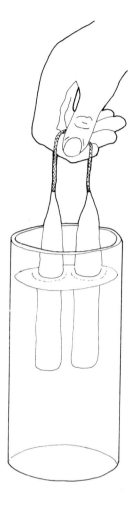

**Figure 5**.  *Hand-dipping a pair of candles*

possible to adapt them to suit individual circumstances. The temperatures and raw materials mentioned are examples of what some people have found to be suitable for their particular situations. Although it is by no means necessary to use the materials mentioned, it is important to remember that different raw materials require different temperatures and times from those mentioned. It will therefore be necessary to experiment with a few candles until you determine the right set of conditions for your situation.

16

1. *Raw ingredients. From left to right: stearine wax block, white wax beads, beeswax beads and beeswax sheets. In the foreground: powdered dye, dye cakes and dye in larger blocks.*

2. *Finished candles. On the left, various sizes of moulded candles. To the right, dipped candles still joined in pairs.*

**3. Dipping**  *Placing wax beads in a 'double boiler' system to make dipped candles. This one is an electrically heated caterer's boiler with a metal vat containing the wax which fits snugly in over the hot water.*

**4. Dipping**  *When the wax reaches the required temperature and is liquid and clear, the artisan dips the measured wicks in the molten wax, then into the water to cool, then hangs the coated wicks on a simple drying frame, ensuring they do not touch.*

**5. Dipping**  *On a small-scale, commercial level, the wicks are prepared by weighting with metal at the ends and threading onto circular wooden dipping boards. (Photo, the author)*

**6. Dipping**  *The wicks are lowered into the molten wax, with mechanical help. (Photo, the author)*

**7. Dipping** *A drying rack, showing its position relative to the artisan dipping the candles. (Photo, the author)*

**8. Dipping** *Cutting loose the finished candles. (Photo, the author)*

**9. Moulding**   *Setting up the wick for a moulded candle. This particular mould is made of glass. The wick is pulled up through the mould using wire, having been primed in the wax below . . .*

**10.** . . . *It is then secured at the top of the mould with wood (or metal) to hold the wick steady.*

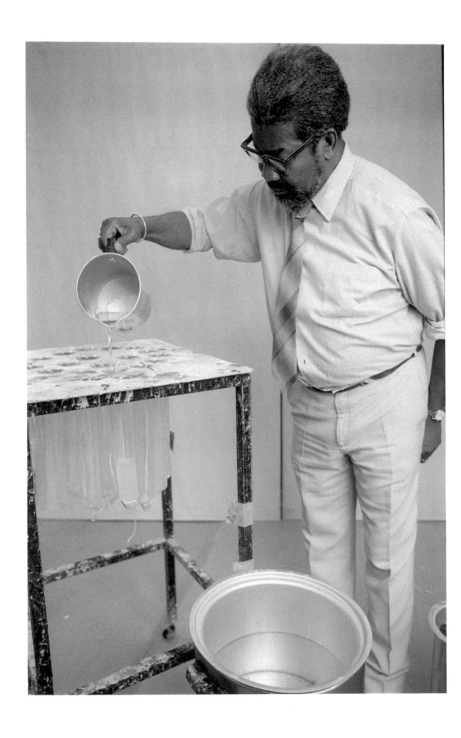

**11.** *Having sealed the moulds at the lower end with bungs of malleable (plasticine-like) material, the hot wax is carefully poured in.*

## Dipping

The equipment used for dipping can range from a stick from which the wicks are suspended to an elaborate, commercially made machine. At the very simplest level, dipping may be carried out by holding the centre of a wick in one hand and dipping it repeatedly into molten wax so that a pair of candles is produced (Figure 5). Although this approach is not usually suitable, as it results in a very low rate of production, it is the principle on which all dipping machinery is based.

In the dipping process, a number of wicks are suspended and repeatedly dipped into molten wax, successive layers being built up to form the finished candle. Excess wax drains off, but some remains at the lower end which is therefore thicker. Although it is possible to produce uniform candles using this method, by discarding the lower 10cm or so, this is wasteful in terms of heat applied and wick used unless the tapered section may also be used as a candle. It may therefore be preferable to use a different technique (such as moulding) if it is necessary to produce only uniform candles.

In order to obtain a well-formed candle, the wick should be submerged in the molten wax and withdrawn as smoothly as possible so that even layers with no drips or other surface imperfections, are built up. The use of a counterweight wherever possible is therefore recommended.

Figure 6 illustrates a continuous dipping process for four or more wick holders suspended from a wheel. Using this method, the wheel is rotated after each dip to enable a fresh set of wicks to be presented for dipping.

Figure 7 illustrates another set of equipment which may also be used to produce dipped candles. In this process, a wick holder is removed from the storage rack and the wicks dipped into the wax using the apparatus shown. It is then returned to the rack to cool, while the remaining holders are dipped in turn. The process is repeated until candles of the required diameter have been produced.

The wax container must be deeper than the length of the longest candle to be made, and should be filled to a level which allows for displacement of the wax during dipping. The container may be heated using any one of the methods described earlier, but as the wax is to be kept at a constant temperature for a considerable time and undergo cooling each time candles are dipped into it, continuous heating, insulation and, ideally, thermostatic controls are advantageous. It may also prove useful to keep a second container filled with wax at the correct temperature. The wax from this container may then be used to top up the first container, so that no time is

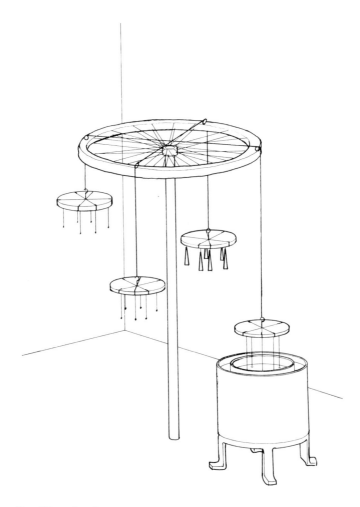

**Figure 6.** *The dipping process using wick holders suspended from a wheel*

wasted in waiting for top up wax to reach the temperature required for dipping.

The correct amount of wax should be weighed and placed in the wax container. The wicks are hung from the wick holders at one end and weighted at the other end. A pin (which is easily visible to the operator) may be used to pierce one wick on each of the holders, so that candles of the right length are produced. It may then be removed when several layers have been built up.

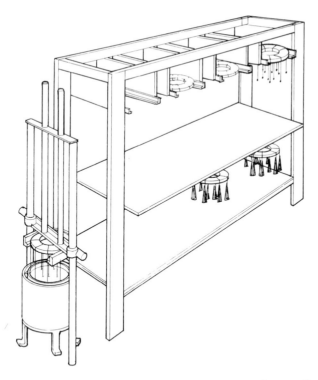

**Figure 7.** *Alternative equipment for larger-scale candle dipping*

## Priming the wicks

When the wax has been heated to the correct temperature (eg 75°C for a blend of 70 per cent paraffin wax and 30 per cent beeswax) the first group of wicks should be lowered into it. They should be left to soak for about three minutes to allow air and moisture to escape. This process is known as priming and should be done with each new group of wicks. The primed wicks should be drawn through the fingers as they cool, so that any lumps are removed. This will help to ensure that the finished candles are smooth and uniform.

When all the wicks have been primed, the dipping proper begins. Each dip should be carried out slowly and smoothly, leaving the wicks immersed in the wax for about five seconds. The group of wicks are then dipped in turn so that by the time all the wicks have been dipped once, the first group of wicks is ready to be dipped for a second time.

In practice, the conditions should be such as to produce the best appearance for the least number of dips per candle. Various factors affect this:

○ increasing the time between dips reduces the number of dips needed;

○ increasing the temperature of the wax increases the number of dips needed;

○ higher air temperature increases the time needed between dips.

When the required thickness has been built up, the candles are removed, trimmed at their lower ends and allowed to cool. An alternative method is to dip the ends in hot water and then to cut the wicks. It is also possible for the weights to be cut from the wicks about two-thirds of the way through the process, as soon as enough wax has been deposited to ensure their shape is kept during dipping. In all cases, any wax which surrounds the weights may be removed and re-melted. The weights themselves may also be re-used. The finished candles may be rolled on a warm glass, metal or stone surface in the same way as poured candles if a very smooth surface is required.

Although the two sets of equipment illustrated enable candles to be produced by what is essentially the same method, they differ in factors such as the materials and skills required for their manufacture, workshop space required, the number of candles which can be produced at any one time and the rates of production which can be achieved.

## Pouring

The equipment used in the pouring process (see Figure 8) is very simple. It consists of an old bicycle wheel in a horizontal plane supported by a vertical shaft, the length of which is determined by a suitable working position. The bottom end of the shaft should be located in a heavy base-plate, to ensure that the apparatus is safe for working. The wheel must be able to rotate freely. Small metal hooks made from thin wire are fixed to the outer rim of the wheel, from which the candle wicks are suspended. The wicks are weighted at their lower ends using, for example, lead. A heated container, similar to that used for dipping, is positioned so that the outer rim of the wheel is above the centre of the container. A small ladle is required for pouring the heated wax over the wick.

The wax is heated to the correct temperature (again, for a blend of 70 per cent paraffin wax and 30 per cent beeswax, a temperature of 75°C is required) and is poured, using the ladle, down each wick in turn. Any wax which drips from the wicks goes back into the melter,

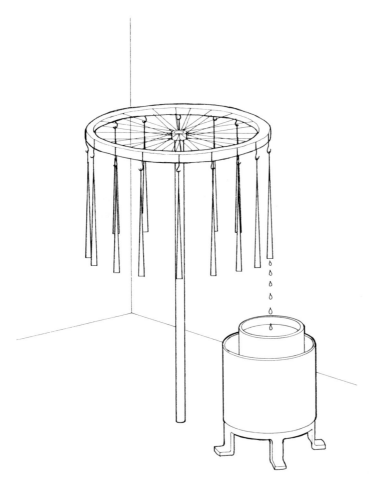

**Figure 8.**   *The pouring process*

although it is possible to arrange for it to drip into a separate container. During pouring, the wick should be twisted slowly to aid the formation of an even coating of wax. After each pouring, the wheel is turned until the next wick is positioned above the wax container and the process is repeated.

It is only possible for a certain amount of wax to be added at each pouring. The candle must therefore be built up from many thin layers; the process being repeated until the required thickness has been built up. It is important that the conditions are right for pouring: if the candles are too warm and the wax is also too hot, one pouring will tend to melt the previous layer. The temperature of the wax should therefore be adjusted to take into account the speed of working round the wheel, the workshop temperature and the composition of the wax mixture.

During the pouring, the candles may sway a little and stick together. If this happens they can be separated gently with a knife, or by tapping.

When a sufficient thickness of wax has been built up, the candles are removed from the wheel and the weights cut off. They can then be rolled smooth on a warm glass or metal surface or stone slab after which they should be hung by their wicks for twenty-four hours to cool.

## *Moulding (or casting)*

Moulding (or casting) is most suitable for the following conditions:
○ for a household which is making candles for its own use, so that the number required is very small;
○ for candles which are decorative rather than strictly utilitarian (in which many techniques of colouring, texturing and the production of special shapes are used);
○ for candles which are over 4cm in diameter;
○ in the mass production of plain candles, in which case special machines are used.

Thus moulding may not be suitable for use on a small industry basis if plain candles are to be produced. The technical reasons for this are that the moulds must be well designed and accurately made if they are to be reliable, that continual attention during cooling is needed for topping up as the wax contracts and that for an output comparable to some of the other candlemaking techniques, a large number of moulds is required. However, the method can produce highly finished and decorative candles.

In general, candle moulds come in two varieties; rigid and flexible. Rigid moulds are made from materials such as metal, glass and plastic whereas flexible moulds are made from rubber or PVC. Flexible moulds can be used to produce irregular-shaped candles.

The techniques described below enable regular-shaped candles to be produced using rigid moulds. They can therefore be used to produce utilitarian candles, or decorative candles using one of the techniques described later.

The technique itself is very simple, consisting of suspending a wick in a mould and then filling the cavity of the mould with molten wax. When the wax has cooled and set, the finished candle can be removed and will be an exact replica of the internal shape of the mould.

It is important that the wick is positioned in the centre of the mould and held taut, for example by tying it to a rod at the top of the mould. Moulds should be sealed at the bottom using either mould sealant (available from craft shops/candlemaking suppliers) or an equivalent substance which will prevent wax from seeping out of the mould. Wicks for use with rigid moulds should be primed first, as described on page 27. Primed wicks aid the removal of mould sealant from the finished candle and ensure that air is excluded from the wick.

A hard paraffin wax (that is one with a melting point of about 60°C to 68°C) is ideal for moulding, as it is less likely to adhere to the sides of the mould than a softer (lower melting point) wax. A relatively high proportion of stearic acid may be added to improve both the hardness of the candle and its shrinkage when cooling; thus aiding the removal of the candle from the mould. A small proportion of microcrystalline wax may also be added; again to improve the hardness, and give a good surface finish to the candle. A blend of waxes of this type will produce a high quality, long-burning candle,

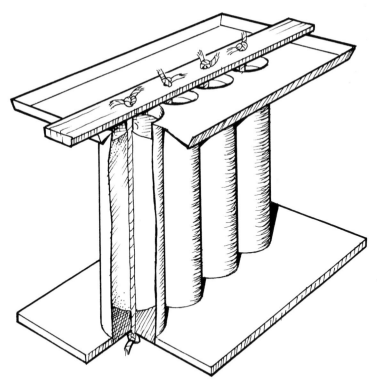

**Figure 9.**  *The moulding process using simple moulds*

31

although it may be possible to produce an adequate candle using paraffin wax alone.

Figure 9 shows a simple set of metal moulds which may be used. It is possible to design a similar set which has a larger or smaller number of moulds than those shown to enable the appropriate number of candles to be produced at one time.

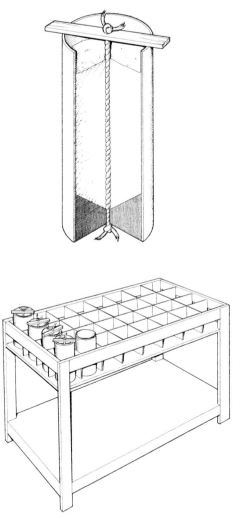

**Figure 10.** *The moulding process – moulds with rack*

Figure 10 shows a more complex arrangement which is capable of producing a relatively large number of candles at one time. The rack can be made either from wood or from metal, but if wood is chosen the surface on which the moulds rest should be covered with a thin sheet of metal, so as to prevent wax from seeping into the wood should a spillage occur. The top half of the rack is divided into rectangular boxes to ensure that the moulds remain upright during pouring. The dimensions of the rack and boxes are dependent on the number of candles to be produced and their size.

The mould shown in Figure 10 is made of metal seamless pipe. It is possible, however, to use any suitable container provided that it can withstand the temperature of the wax and has a smooth, parallel inside surface to ensure easy removal of the finished candle. The bung may be made from wood (in which case allowance must be made for seepage which will occur initially) or metal (in which case it must be fabricated from a metal which is no harder than that from which the mould is made).

The wax, heated to a temperature between 80°C and 88°C, is poured into the mould and allowed to cool slowly. As the wax cools it shrinks, so the top surface of the wax must be broken at intervals and topped up. This prevents the formation of a candle with air holes in it. However, it is important to top up only as high as the original level of the wax, as otherwise the surplus wax seeps between the cooling candle and its mould, producing a candle with a poor surface finish.

It is possible to immerse the moulds in cold water to increase the rate of cooling, although it is important to wait for a few minutes after pouring before doing this. It is also necessary to ensure that the water level is higher than the wax level in the moulds, so that the whole candle is cooled rather than just a part of it, but at the same time to prevent water from getting inside the moulds. Wooden racks are not suitable for immersing in water. The moulds should be removed from the water when topping-up. When the wax has cooled and set, the finished candle can be removed from the mould and should be an exact replica of the internal shape of the mould. One of the advantages of using this method is that it produces candles with a good surface finish which need no further processing.

# 4. Producing decorative candles

It is possible to make decorative candles from candles produced using the techniques outlined in this book. Some methods require that the candle first be overdipped with coloured wax, where other methods can be used with ordinary white candles. In all cases, it is best to plan the design (on paper for example) before starting to work with the candle.

## Dyeing

One of the most common ways of producing a decorative candle is to use colour. It is possible to make coloured candles in two ways:
o by dyeing the wax before making the candles, so that 'solid' coloured candles are produced;
o by overdipping plain white candles with layers of brightly coloured wax. The addition of a small amount of fat to the paraffin wax (for example stearine or beeswax) is necessary to obtain bright colours.
It is possible to use either dyes or pigments (or, in certain situations, a combination of both) to colour candle wax. The amount of dyestuff required per kilogram (kg) of wax should be recommended by the supplier. However, as the amount of colouring material required to give a particular shade is dependent on the composition of the wax mixture, this figure should be used as a guide only, and different proportions of dyestuff be used until the required shade is obtained. In general, a much greater proportion of dyestuff is required for over-dipping than for producing 'solid' coloured candles.

## Painting

This technique involves the use of a very strongly dyed wax to paint a design on to the surface of a candle with a paint brush. The technique can be used to produce designs ranging from very simple to extremely complex ones.

## Dried flowers and grasses

A very effective way of decorating a plain white candle is to use dried flowers or grasses. It is necessary to have pressed the flowers some time in advance so that they have dried completely before being used on the candle.

After each piece of the design has been placed on the candle, it is necessary to press it on using a hot metal object such as a spatula or a spoon handle. When the design has been completed, the candle must be dipped into hot wax two or three times to seal it in.

It is possible to use many other natural artifacts (shells, for example) to decorate candles. The opportunities are limited only by the resources available, and your imagination.

## *Carving*

Wax is a fairly soft substance and is therefore easy to carve. Although it is possible to carve a design into a single colour candle, the effect of carving can be seen best on a candle with different coloured layers. It is possible to overdip an ordinary white candle several times to build up layers of coloured wax and, after the candle has cooled completely, to carve a design in the wax. It is best to remove a little wax at a time using a sharp knife, as this gives greater control over the final design.

Designs can range from simple round or oval shapes cut out of a candle to reveal different coloured layers, to highly ornate designs. However it is important to remember not to cut so deeply into the candle so as to expose the wick or make it unstable when burning.

# Appendices

## Appendix I Common problems

When a candle or set of candles is not quite right it is important to discover the reason in order to prevent the problem recurring. There is usually a simple explanation. Some common problems are outlined in Table 3 below, with probable causes and suggested action to avoid their recurrence. In the event of a serious fault which cannot be easily remedied, the candle can often be re-melted and another one formed without the original fault.

**Table 3**

| Problem | Cause | Action |
| --- | --- | --- |
| Smoky candle | Wick is too large | Use a smaller wick |
| | Candle in a draught | Ensure candle is not in a draught when lit |
| | Wick requires trimming | Trim wick |
| Candle goes out | Wick is too small (large pool of molten wax) | Use a larger wick |
| Candle drips | Wick is too small | Use a larger wick |
| *Moulded candles*<br>Candle cannot be removed from mould | Inappropriate mould used (singe piece, rigid moulds must be able to withstand high temperatures, have smooth interior surfaces and parallel sides or top (open) end wider than bottom (sealed) end | Re-melt the candle, use a different mould |
| | Paraffin wax with too low a melting point and/or not enough stearine used | Run hot water over sides of mould and re-melt (altering wax composition) if necessary |
| | Wax 'topped up' above original level in mould, causing seepage between candle and mould | Run hot water over sides of mould and re-melt candle if necessary |
| | Candle cooled too slowly | Run hot water over sides of mould, or place in cool place to aid contraction. Re-melt candle if necessary |

**Table 3 (cont'd.)**

| Problem | Cause | Action |
|---|---|---|
| Bubbles at or near base of candle | Level of water bath lower than level of wax in mould | Fill bath with more water next time |
| Thermal cracks in candle | Candle has cooled too quickly (water in bath too cold?) | |
| | 'Topping up' wax too hot | |
| | 'Topping up' done too late so candle has cooled too much | |
| Candle splutters/goes out/fails to light | Water got into candle from inadequately sealed mould | |

## Appendix II Conversion factors

**Length**
1 centimetre (cm) = 10 millimetres (mm)
1 centimetre is approximately equal to 0.4 inches
So: 4cm = 1.5 inches
    10cm = 4 inches

**Temperature**
In order to convert temperatures in °F to °C, use the following formula:

$$C = (F - 32) \times \frac{5}{9}$$

and to convert temperatures in °C to °F, use the following formula:

$$F = \frac{9}{5}C + 32$$

C = temperatures in °C
F = temperatures in °F


## Appendix III Suppliers of raw materials and equipment

Bayer UK Ltd
Bayer House
Strawberry Hill
Newbury
Berkshire
UK (dyes)

BP France
10 quai Paul Doumer
92412 Courbevoir Cedex
France (paraffin wax)

Candle Makers Supplies
28 Blythe Road
London W14 OHA
UK (craft suppliers)

Croda Universal Ltd
Cowick Hall
Snaith
Goole
N Humberside DN14 9AA
UK (stearine)

Hayes and Finch Ltd
Hanson Road
Long Lane
Aintree
Liverpool L9 7BP
UK (wicks)

ICI Organics Division
Hexagon House
Blakely
Manchester M9 3DA
UK (dyes and pigments)

Unichema Chemicals Ltd
Bebington
Wirral
Merseyside L62 4UF
UK (stearine)

University of California
Division of Agricultural Sciences
1422 Harbour Way South
Richmond
CA 94804
USA (information on making a solar wax melter)

Yarncraft
Three Ply House
57A Lant Street
London SE1 1QN
UK (cotton for wicks)